TABLE OF CONTENTS

THE DESTINY CYCLE

LEAVING THE LIFE SOCIETY ASSIGNED TO YOU

BY

ANTHONY BROWN

Brown / DESTINY CYCLE / 6

INTRODUCTION

I've heard so many things in my life. Words have power, the ability to frame images in one's mind. As human beings we have the ability, some would even say the gift, to actually use these images as a guidepost to influence our direction in life. In this way, words have the ability to bypass our instinctual nature and alter our path away from or align us towards our destiny. Animals act by instinct. When they need to urinate they just do in a way that their instinct dictates. They don't do it by suggestion. They don't wait for the opportune time, or reject the notion because a bathroom isn't sanitary enough, they just go. When an animal is hungry, they just kill and eat…no menus are presented to them for scrutiny and selectivity.

Destiny is governed by spiritual instinct. It's the end result of manifested purpose. It is not governed or shaped by society's development, influence, technology, laws, or morality. It is governed by God or the Divine. In this book I will refer to the Divine as S.A.M (Sam).

Why? Because Spirit Adores Me, Spirit Amplifies Me, and Spirit Affirms Me. I want to acknowledge those 3 things whenever I refer to the Divine in my life. Not a gimmick, a slogan, or a focal point…just a loving way to strengthen myself as I write this book.

Back to Destiny. Here's an example of it in action. Last night, on my way home I decided to pick up dinner. I grounded myself and thought about of what I wanted to eat. I then focused and opened myself up to what Sam would want me to have. Yes, I actually consult Sam for things as trivial as that…and I often don't listen to his suggestions, as my Heineken gut would attest to. A little note, a suggestion is the lowest form of energetic speech because it implies that whatever was said didn't resonate with enough power and intention to inspire one hundred percent support from the person listening. When you receive direction from Sam in response to asking for direction in life follow it as an imperative, not a suggestion.

I saw a vision of what I wanted to eat…a steak sandwich and ice cream for dessert. I heard Sam tell me to get the steak sandwich from my favorite fast food spot in town at the time, Spiros, and go to 7-Eleven for

ice cream. Not an audible voice, just a quiet directive. I was told to go to

the 7-Eleven off of 9th Street and Gaffey in San Pedro, the city I live in. I

usually go to the location off of 19th and Pacific but for some reason I was

hearing Sam tell me to go to the other location. I took this aspect of Sam's

purpose for me as a suggestion and decided to go to my normal location.

When I stepped into the store I didn't feel right about it but ignored that

sign. I walked back to the frozen products section and headed towards the

ice cream. There were no prices listed by the flavor I liked, none listed at

all for any of the brand I usually buy. The containers had some kind of

gook on them. It was sticky and gross. The inside had been contaminated

with air because they had hollow sections I could feel within them when I

squeezed the outside of the container. This usually happens when the

freezer section is defrosted. This is done for routine maintenance but the

side effect is that all frozen products that were in the freezer either

partially or fully melt. When the freezer is brought back down to optimal

temperature the texture and consistency of the products they house

change. This is what happened in this case. I was almost ready to buy a

flavor I didn't want just to get what appeared to be an undamaged pint when I thought to myself, "Sam told me to go to the other location, maybe I should just head there". In life society gives us a pre-determined path to take which often is totally counterintuitive to our own spiritual instinct and intuition. We don't have to take it.

I left the 7-Eleven on Pacific and 19th and went to the one on 9th and Gaffey. I walked into the frozen product section and headed for the ice cream. They had the flavor I wanted, <u>Caramel Cone</u>. They had prices, actually it was on sale for 2 for $7.99. Usually one pint was almost six dollars.

Here's how this event breaks down in the context of what my book relates to:

1. I first **_grounded_** myself then decided I wanted to get dinner on the way home.

2. I then **_focus_**ed and asked Sam to tell me what I should eat.

3. I felt the **_power_** from the vision and intention I received from Sam

4. This power translates into a given **_purpose_** for accomplishing that goal.

5. I began to *act* on the directives within that purpose received.

6. I reaped the *results* or manifestation of the actions taken

Grounded, Focus, Power, Purpose, Act, Results…

I call this process the Destiny Cycle and although it's a great way to find an awesome deal on my desired flavor of ice cream, there's a greater meaning in its application. When we follow the path society has prescribed for us irrespective of spiritual intuition and instinct, we can end up where I did, at the wrong 7-Eleven. A horrible thought, I know.

My desire is for every human being to be self-aware, one-ness minded, and directed by Sam. Living in the Destiny Cycle leads to this state of living.

I am an intuitive coach that specializes in dating and relationship, health and wellness, communication and effectivity, and diet and exercise. Although I have prior experience and training in all these areas I am not certified in any one. I don't hold a degree in any related field and will never claim a reference point of expertise based on society's definition of such. My background is one hundred percent reliant on my trust in Sam. The principles I espouse are based on my spiritual instinct and intuition. This book is about self-awareness and empowerment. Without those two qualities in operation in your life, no title, degree, certification, medal, or award will have much meaning. I'm not going to prescribe an antidote for anything, not going to cure any cancer, not going to tell you the secret of life's existence. I am going to, however, lead you into a world that few people understand with any resonance. I'm going to help you understand why when you were 5 minutes late to work and you thought that your character and reputation were shot…that actually you avoided a car accident that would have made you being on time irrelevant because you would have been dead. I'm going to assist you in knowing yourself enough to make a decision as to which friend to call in a crisis when every second counts. I'm going to teach you to develop the muscle of your spiritual intuition and instinct, some people call it your third eye. Let's just say it's a different form of perception. If that is of no interest to you, no offense taken. If you, however, want a level of self-awareness, drive, and success you've never had before, read on.

Here is a quick glossary of terms for the reader. This will greatly assist in understanding the flow and processes in The Destiny Cycle. Although I believe the concepts laid out are true you may see and interpret them however you feel best suits the integrity of the method prescribed.

Divinity - I describe the universal source of life, energy and manifestation as either Sam, The Divine, God, Allah, Jesus, or Love.

Spirit - The part of you that directly aligns to and is one with Source

Heart - The passionate place that connects your spirit's vision to your soul's imperative

Soul - The subconscious, invisible mind

Mind - The conscious, physical mind

Body - The physical body that the mind commands

I believe there are some concepts that resonate with the soul directly and have no understanding in the conscious mind. I believe there are concepts of this nature within this book so I urge every reader to keep an open heart so that the messages that are of this nature can impact you spiritually. The spirit of who we are, I believe, points to the one-ness that

gives us are real reason for being, which is to love one another.

CHAPTER 1

GROUNDED

Establishing a Home Base

The first step in the Destiny Cycle is being grounded. I look at grounding as the act of being present spiritually, mentally and physically in any space you inhabit. This sounds so natural in concept. In application it can be difficult for a lot of people. Our minds are bombarded with so many thoughts that distract, our bodies constantly processing a multitude of ailments/impulses/stimulus, and our souls are often so disconnected from the true spiritual nature of who we are. This in turn separates us from one-ness, our universal understanding of the love we must give, receive and be, individually. Getting ourselves grounded starts with re-connecting our soul with its assigned spirit. This takes place in the heart.

The soul, or unconscious mind can get lost when it receives its directives from the bottom up verses the top down. The soul was meant to be directed by its spirit's vision, not by its body's ailment. The heart must be clear and open to keep this connection flowing. The heart of a person is where their soul and spirit meet, connect, and exchange. The vision of Sam is translated through the focused beam of your own unique spirit. This powerful love resonates in the heart. Our heart must know it's loved to remain open and resonant and store that love. The first understanding that a person must actively acknowledge is that he or she is loved by God and his or her own spirit. After this is done then the heart is active and ready to receive and house that love. Your soul can now access this love at full power and resonance from its heart.

Acknowledge that you are loved by Sam and that you love yourself. Now acknowledge that you are to give to, receive from and be that love for others. In the bible, and many other religious texts, it states that God is Love. If God is Love and we are manifestations of His Love then it stands to reason that we can be love. Now that your heart is resonating with that truth, your soul can access the power of it. When I say love, in the lower case, I express it in terms of the love we exchange as translated through the unique loving beings we are. This love has our signature or expression on it. When I speak of Love, in the uppercase, I mean the fact that all love, in every expression points back to and is universally a part of God's

Love. Now your spirit and soul are re-connected via your heart, and therefor grounded through that alignment. Now let's get your mind ready to respond to and follow your soul's powerful imperative.

Our conscious thought processes comprise the mind. The mind translates thoughts into manifest actions. Those actions bring results. The physical body doesn't move, breathe, jump, run, cry, sleep, or laugh without a manifest command initiated from the mind. To get your mind clear and focused is an act of your conscious will. It is entirely possible and human beings have been doing it for thousands of years. To clear your mind you have to be the master of it. This isn't as hard as it sounds and we, from birth, as human beings, have had this capacity. Meditation is one of the key ways to settle the mind to a central thought or idea and resonate at its frequency. Another action that clears the mind is exercise. Exercise helps you sleep better for this reason because it settles the mind, especially when meditation is combined with exercise, for example in martial arts or yoga. Clearing your mind can also be as simple as picking a focal point or specific visualization until nothing else exists in your thoughts.

I have several tattoos. I would always prepare myself mentally for the pain of being tattooed by meditating on a focal point in my surrounding space. I would look up at the ceiling, and pick a particular feature and stare at it. It could be a bump in the acoustic tile, or a crack. In order to do this successfully you have to be mentally present in the space you inhabit. With a clear and present mind I could then tell my body that the pain I was about to feel was accepted by me.

Visualize yourself as a tree with your roots planted deep in the ground. See those roots reach deep down while focusing on your spirit-soul affirmation about giving, receiving and being love. Now your mind should resonate with the same peace that your soul and spirit share, creating a grounded state. This brings us to our last aspect of the grounding process, settling the body and bringing it into cooperation and alignment with your mind's peace.

The body follows the mind, always. The body is an extension of the mind's will and aspiration. Whatever the mind aspires to accomplish, it commands the body to carry out actions necessary to doing so. Emotions are included in this. For the mind to express an emotion appropriately and with outside recognition, the body has to exhibit the appropriate physical language, movement and expression to facilitate understanding. If you wanted to cry, but laughed instead that could be looked at as an inappropriate body translation of your minds will and aspiration. Use your clear mind to command a cooperative and receptive state in your body. This is why staying in good physical condition is imperative to fulfilling one's destiny. Your body is a tool for creativity and manifestation but if you render it useless through poor diet and lack of exercise than there will be things that you are called to do and places you are assigned to be, that you will not be able to accomplish or be present for in this life. Use your clear and centered mind to tell your body to be at peace with and adhere to whatever vision and guidance it gives.

Take deep breaths…two or three. Sit or stand in a comfortable place if possible, free from a lot of outside, disruptive stimulus. Focus your 5 senses on fully receiving whatever passionate imperative your mind expresses. Now your spirit, soul, mind and body are present and receptive and you are grounded.

I spent many years not being grounded in anything in particular. When I was a child my mother was an astrologer and numerologist. My father is Christian and came from a long line of Baptist ministers. I had a lot of different concepts coming at me from many directions. Despite this I had my own calling, my own spiritual intuition and instinct that manifested often as my mother re-tells it. She spoke of one account from my childhood where she and my grandmother were in a Volkswagen bug with me in the car seat in the back when the car broke down. That apparently was a big deal back in the day as there were no cell phones or AAA that I'm aware of, at least we couldn't afford it if there was. She says I was 3. According to her account she and my grandmother began to freak out and go into distress. Then I somehow got free out of my car seat and started to scream from the rear window, "Friends, where are you friends! We need you friends, we need you!!!" This especially startled my mother because I spoke very little at the time and when I did it wasn't that articulate. Someone came and helped us.

I had a sense of something inside myself, a gift to understand that support came from more sources than could be seen or sensed under normal circumstances. I had a sense of my connection to something spiritual. My mother has many stories like this that she has shared. I don't really remember them but she does.

The first time I ever felt grounded was when I preached for the first time. I sat down in the front row of church and prepared my spirit to speak. I just kept focusing on the message I was hearing in that moment even though I had already written a message and prepared all week. I was grounding myself and didn't even realize it. I said to myself, "God, I only want you to speak through me, no one else. I don't want to express my own feelings, just yours. I want to love and help people." I felt the Love of God envelope me. I then became full of peace in the midst of an energy storm. The energy was in the form of the words that were preparing to articulate out of my spirit's love, via my soul's powerful imperative through my mind's passionate command of my mouth's vocal resonance. I had never grounded myself like this to generate this much power but I felt the difference with it tangibly. Preaching the gospel was a revelation to me. The act of speaking into other people's lives and enriching them spiritually made my heart full and still does. It's deeper than the gospel, deeper than words. It was the subconscious awareness that as human beings we need to love one another to be happy. We need to acknowledge our one-ness to each other.

Grounding is the act of loving yourself as you are in the present moment. Never wait on loving yourself, never pass the opportunity ahead to the future or be too weighed down by the past to love yourself in the present. To love yourself in the present, you have to be present spiritually, mentally and physically. This act causes you to create a home base from wherever you are because your spirit roots itself in the soil of that present moment's purpose. In this way home really is where your heart is because proximity doesn't matter anymore. If we are too static in how we establish a home base then whenever life upends us we will cower and submit to the fear of the unknown. If we root our spirit in the moment however, we realize that this earth is our home, the galaxy is our home, and the universe is our home. Where we can go is only limited by how far we can expand our spirit. Every other aspect of us has limits. I'm thankful that my mother moved so much when I was a child. I used to resent it but now I see that it developed in me an adaptability and awareness of the truth that home is where your love resides, not your body. When grounded, one establishes a home base of resonance from which to focus his or her spirit's loving vision, into their respective soul's powerful imperative. And you wondered what doing something from the heart felt like, now you know.

Each morning I wake up happy

I sing from my spirit's pride

I soar to new heights because my heart is willing

I listen to the resonance of my soul's tide

I understand that only this moment is promised

My mind aspires to reach its destiny's prize

My goal is to know my love's name…and to see where my one-ness lies

Anthony Brown-2015

CHAPTER 2

FOCUS

Being Your Own Channel

This is where a coach would normally follow the normal path of least resistance and give you the tools to enable you to channel the focus you need to follow your purpose in life. The thing is I'm not normal, never have been. The way I see it, if you can't do it for yourself than what's the point. I need you just as much as you need me. I rely on your powerful connection to Sam just as much as you rely on mine. What I'm going to do is help you understand that you are your own conductor for your own power. You initiate the process of channeling Sam's love and power through you, not me. This in turn gives you a focused beam of your own directed power that leads right into your purpose.

Here's a way to visualize this process. See yourself as a lens. Lenses amplify and focus light. Now see the sun as that light. Our sun radiates light and warmth and is a symbol for life giving sustainment to the Milky Way galaxy. What an amazing star we have in the sun. Astrology is based on planetary spatial alignment in the sky. The sun's alignment

spatially in relationship to a given constellation is the basis for the

meaning and characteristics associated with our sun sign, which is our

birth sign. The study of the significance of the stars and space predates

many religions and associated mythologies. Now see the sun's rays

passing through the lens of who you are as a unique creation, which you

are. As those rays pass through you they are focused into a beam of

immense power and potential. This beam lands at a certain place in time

and space and begins to burn a hole into the place where it lands and

leaves a mark of reference. Now let's go deeper. The sun's rays represent

love and power of Sam. Maybe the sun's rays represent Christ. Maybe

they represent Buddha. Maybe they represent Allah. In astrology, the sun

is the self. The name doesn't matter, but the principle is critical. I mean

no disrespect to those that ascribe more meaning to the name than the

principle behind this visualization. Just remember that spirituality is about

one-ness, not separation. Here is how this vision manifests for the purpose

of the Destiny Cycle.

"The Power and Love of Sam radiates through the lens of who you are which results in a focused beam of your own personal power that lands on and reveals your purpose"

The lens of who you are is another way of describing your spirit. Seeing your spirit as a lens for the purpose of this visualization helps to lead into the focusing aspect of this exercise. This purpose revealed by the focused beam created could be for the moment, the day, the week, or the year. The focusing process is important because in that focus is the personal power needed to fulfill the action associated with the purpose given. Many miss the mark in this area. I, myself included in past pursuits. Here is an example in poetic form.

Ever give some time to a thought that had merit

The idea came like a flash, so powerful you didn't want to scare it

The who was you, the what was exciting, but the how was faint and unclear

*Your **drive** begins to wane and your thought's betray that which, a moment ago, you held so dear...*

The power of an idea provides the **drive** needed to act on its purpose and see it through to its manifested result. The Destiny Cycle breaks down for many people because they fail to focus and direct the love and power of Sam into their own sustained, powerful purpose.

In order to receive and sustain power we must be open to receive the love and power of Sam in our lives. Sam is my personal affirmation. It means Spirit Adores Me, Spirit Amplifies Me and Spirit Affirms Me. It is a constant acknowledgment of what the Divine has done for me every moment, through every breath, in every circumstance, throughout my life. It's not a religious mantra, or a catchphrase. It's my gift to me as I write this book. In order to ground yourself you have to know God loves you. In order to focus you have to let God amplify your own spirit's inspiration with that love. In turn His power amplifies and defines your own personal power. This power drives your soul's imperative. Focus is key in generating enough power to sustain this drive. There is no purity of purpose without the power focus generates.

I started writing a long time ago. Anyone who writes knows the nature of it. It can be drudgery if you don't have a directed purpose. This requires focus. It always started as inspiration for me. Inspiration from an idea or thought. I would focus on receiving the full potential and direction for that thought. Then I would be filled with a drive I couldn't explain. This first happened to me when I was a teenager. I received an inspiration to write a book about manhood. I felt a void in that area of my life at the time and wanted to write about what I thought that was. I didn't have a computer at the time and couldn't type a lick. I started writing. I would write until my hand hurt. I wrote for 10 hours at a time with very small breaks to eat. I had fifty hand written pages done in a few days. It meant something to me and Sam knew it. My concepts were far out to say the least. It was raw, had crude language, and I'm sure spoke in altruistic terms and was very static philosophically. What I remember the most was not the book itself but the energy I received to write it. It seemed to never end and I felt like sleep was my enemy, like it got in the way. As I write this book I feel the same way. I need to write this book. It's not about trying to convince anyone of anything. It's not about changing the world although maybe concepts expressed in it might. It's about receiving an inspiration from God and feeling the drive to stay in the purpose of what it is, and what it means. As a Life and Relationship Coach I've taught my clients many concepts. When I taught this one my heart soared, but my mind lagged behind my heart's enthusiasm. I was teaching this to a client who was in the process of running from my teachings. I had grown to really care about this dude and he was shitting on that care in my opinion. I was like, "He's running from manhood, fuck him". I was just plain pissed about it. I know now that he gave me the greatest gift that I have ever received from a client. The gift of human-ness. The gift of frailty and confusion. I gave him the Destiny Cycle as an afterthought. I intuitively came up with it to keep him from crashing into a brick wall of disappointment and frustration in life. Within 24 hours of teaching him this concept his energy shifted and his life took off. He's an awesome guy and didn't need me to grow and be free in his spirit. I needed him. I needed someone to reach out to me and pull this concept out of my spiritual intuition and instinct. I need everyone who reads this book. I need everyone and everyone needs me. It actually hurts for me to say that. It hurts for me to understand that people I grew to hate in life I need. It hurts to know that people that I have hurt in the past needed me.

Understanding one-ness is seeing that forgiveness of self and others comes from the understanding that when someone does something to harm you, he's harming himself just as much because we all are of one Love. An eternal Love that feeds our human spirit that resides within the walls of the home we call our body but simultaneously has a reach and connectivity we can't fathom.

You know you're focusing when whatever thought, idea, concept, or philosophy you receive from Sam amplifies as it resonates in you and an insatiable hunger develops to see it through to its manifested result. This focus provides the power a world class athlete needs to push his/her body past its limit to breakthrough into a new performance standard. This focus leads a woman, who has been treated with deceit while living in detestable conditions, to stand up and realize she deserves better. With no outward support she launches from within into the unknown to discover her true destiny. This is the focus that caused me to follow a God that I didn't know, a God I was systematically taught to hate, into an adventure that has been an awe-inspiring joy. I asked God to direct my life in my early 20's. I asked him to give me the vision and awareness of who He was and who I was in Him. I submitted my choice to His will in my life. His name, His nature, His purpose and His joy are all locked up in the spirit of His love. This leading of His Eternal Spirit into our own spirit translates us into a freedom that is unexplainable. This freedom comes from discovering our purpose through the power that resonates through our focus.

In the middle of the night

My eyes wide open, sleep escapes and takes flight

I am restless, anxious, resisting with all my might

The voice I hear saying "Be still"

I am overcome with the purpose in the sound of its whisper and soft breath

I open my heart to the power of its rising tone and growing heft

I can't see its urgency, but my focus won't allow its death

The meaning of its travel grows, in me it filters through my soul's prose

I must watch where its message falls

The power of its travel through me has broken down my walls

My understanding at first is faint and small

Then I read my heart's translation because His love has amplified it

though my lens

The Joy of the Lord is My Strength…

Anthony Brown-2015

CHAPTER 3

POWER

The Food of the Soul

Love is the food of the spirit. It gives us the power to remain in oneness with one another. Passion is the food of the mind. It gives tangible energy to our purpose's directive. Now our mind can command our body effectively in fulfilling our original spirit's vision. Power is the food that our soul receives from our focused energy that transmits from Sam through the focused lens of who we are. Let's talk more about "Soul" power.

We have all heard a friend say this haven't we? "I feel it in my soul". What they were saying is that the thought, idea, or concept expressed had a resonance for them. A power behind it that they couldn't explain, not just a notion for them but a mantra or fire inside of them. This is the power. The power that will drive them past negative opinions, criticism, skepticism, and opposition. This power drives them past their own mind's resistance to get their concept out and released with purity. The power keeps the concept pure so it flows into and is clearly reflected in whatever purpose is set for it. People fail in life because they leave their soul out of their pursuits. You can't manifest your destiny in this life without the soul. We skip it all the time by translating Sam's love through us without power because with great power comes great responsibility. That's not just a line from the movie Spiderman 2, it's actually the truth. The responsibility of power is to direct your purpose into a clearly defined path. Otherwise it's dangerous and can be manipulated into a different and sometimes darker purpose. If you don't feel whatever you're receiving from Sam in your soul, then it's not coming from Sam at all and has no power. Don't translate someone else's dream into a destructive force, follow your own and manifest its purpose purely for all to benefit from. Sam's love, as it radiates through your lens, will define its own direction and path. Watch it, feel the joy of living in it and witness it transform and align you to the unique, powerful being you are. One-ness means you see the commonality, not the division in a scenario. It takes power to see the one-ness between us. It takes power to understand that when you say the glass is half empty or half full you're not differentiating between 2 types of human philosophy, one lesser or greater . Both perspectives assess the same thing. It's not different, just two unique perspectives of the same

truth. Power dissipates the reach of social programming and cultural bias

and reveals the purity and clarity in a situation, philosophy or ideology.

Our soul's need the amplified power we receive through our lens from

Sam to define our destiny's imperative with resonance.

I listen to Sam. He speaks to me because I'm open to receive from

Him. That's different from just hearing. Receiving from someone

required that you receive the power in whatever they are saying, not just

the words. The words are the empty carriers without the power present

and the hidden intent they house. If you're a man and a woman says she

wants to work with you and smiles seductively, her intent defines her

purpose, not the words alone. If she says it and hands you a business card

and walks away it could just mean she wants to collaborate with you on a

work-related project. If you look on the back of the card and it has her

personal cellphone number and the room number of the suite she's staying

in then you know she wants to fuck. You know because her business

number is on the front of that card. She didn't have to give you any

personal info at all. She is leading you by leaving a treasure map to glory.

She's saying call me when you're ready to have some fun; here is where

that fun resides. Look at the front of that business card as the words in a

conversation, any conversation. It introduces her presence and identity

into your consciousness. To understand what her intent is or the intent of

any words you hear, tune into the intent and power behind the words

which are the personal info on the back of the business card. With that

information, you have the **"Power"** to act on the purpose of those words.

Without that information you're in the dark as to the true meaning of that

alluring woman's statement. Absent this power, you will never be able to

fully understand your appropriate action in any scenario faced because the

power of the soul drives the passion of the minds intent. The body follows

the passionate resonance of our mind's command. The subconscious mind

is the soul's command center. It uses it to translate the focused power it

receives from Sam's love into a purposed set of commands for the

conscious mind and body to follow. This is why it's so imperative that

you keep your subconscious mind clear through prayer and meditation. If

it's full of self-doubt, hate, divisiveness and schisms you won't be open to

receive the Love of God in purity. You'll skew it to and filter it through the subconscious beliefs that have been implanted in you from society thus diluting Sam's power and ultimately tainting His message.

If your soul receives the power from Sam's love and the focused message is "Exercise more so you can prepare yourself to run a 10k", you are responsible to physically exercise in accordance with that messages purpose. What if after focusing you decide to ignore the message's intent and you say to yourself, "I have an old injury that makes running uncomfortable and not feasible". You block the message's power at the soul level to fuel the necessary passion your mind needs to direct the body. You wake up the next day with a renewed desire to run because you know the message was from Sam. You get dressed in running shorts and a T-Shirt and notice that your ankle hurts from the old injury you referenced in your mind the previous day when you first heard Sam's message. You then receive a text from your ex-boyfriend or girlfriend saying he or she wants to come over for a quickie before work. You say, "I'll do it tomorrow", and make a choice to save your ankle by doing some sexual gymnastics instead of running. Then you injure your ankle even more during that supremely enjoyable act, tweak it real bad, and make running impossible. Or so you think. Then you still receive the same message from Sam, day after day, but choose to ignore it because now you have a real excuse for not running.

Sam was preparing you for a 10k that was going to take place within one month. The race location was about a quarter-mile down the road from where you live. You wouldn't have been ready for this 10k in a month but Sam wanted you to prepare for it anyway. Recently you had been talking to a friend about how hard it was to find a mate and how you never seem to be in the right place at the right time. Sam heard you. He set up a meet and greet with a man or woman that you would have a fulfilling 10-year relationship with. You would meet at that 10k. It was going to go something like this, from a female perspective:

"I was prepping for a 10k; I don't know why really…just had a bug up my ass to do it one morning. I hadn't even picked a particular event or location yet, just felt led to start running. I found a 10k that was taking place within a month. It was only 3 blocks from my house so I was stoked about it. I trained hard but was nowhere near ready to run it when the day came. I had been nursing an old ankle injury for years, it was inflamed on race day, but I just had this unexplainable drive to do this. At the

starting point just before the gun shot off I released my inhibitions and just

ran. About halfway through I physically couldn't run anymore so I started

to walk. Then I started to cry. I was a hot mess. Then I heard a voice. It

was coming from behind me and getting closer. The person behind me

wasn't running, but walking and not at a rushed pace I might add. A

handsome gentlemen with a bald head and no eyebrows. Piercing blue

eyes, about 6ft tall. His body was not optimal but something about him

made me smile big. He said "Hi I'm Frank, are you ok?" I said I was in

pain but wasn't going to quit. I asked him to walk with me. I don't know

why I asked this to this day but I'm glad I did. He said it would be his

pleasure. He said I had a beautiful spirit, that he couldn't help but notice

me. He was all wrong and weird looking but so damn handsome at the

same time. He says to me, "I just found out that my brain cancer is in

remission, my treatments were successful. I was so excited and overjoyed

about it that I decided to run this 10k on inspiration alone, kind of a bad

idea, lol!" I started to cry again. This guy was incredible and I realized

that part of why he was walking with me was to encourage himself to keep

going as much as he was encouraging me. That's how we met. We've been together for over 8 years now, best years of my life. His cancer came back a few months ago and he's not responding to treatment. Doctor says a few months to a year and a half at best. This man saved my life and now all I can think about every moment of every day is how I wish I could save his. When I get down he just says that every breath he gets to inhale in my presence is a gift from God and heals him for the next breath. I love this man".

Sam wants the best for you. He sees what you can't. In his Love and power is the answer to your heart's request. When you're vulnerable and submit yourself to be a lens so he can pour his love and power through you it creates a focused beam of your own personal power that directs you to and gives you the drive to walk out your purpose with action. It starts with grounding yourself. Then you submit to focus. Then you receive power. That power gives you the drive to fulfill your purpose. This defined purpose leads to action. The action leads to a result or manifest destiny. Don't cut the power off and disable your soul's imperative that you receive from the focused love of the Divine. Don't doubt yourself, follow the message as you hear it and follow the path of the power given to complete its purpose.

Your spirit's food is **Love**

Your soul's food is **Power**

Your mind's food is **Passion**

Your body's food is a **double cheese burger with extra pickles**…lighten up people, just

because I'm in tears right now doesn't mean you have to be.

We eat to make sure the body has the fuel it needs to physically act on the mind's commands. Exercise causes the body to excel at completing these commands through repetition and practice. That means exercise to manifest destiny, not just to manifest a 6-pack!

What if I was like Gravity?

What if all things that came towards me were drawn to the center of my heart…verses the center of the Earth?

What if a man's hand in need was undeniably drawn to the center of my

supply?

What if the power behind the force that holds me together, held the

universe in place

Understand my strength, for the power behind it connects me too the love

in your spirit's expression

How can we see power as its own end…and not feel its direction to a

purposed destination

What if the thought of my mind's passion relieved a man's depression and

grounded him in joy

If the love of my soul's vision could somehow feed the need of the masses

poverty

How can the power behind that love be revealed?

Through my soul's cry…my soul and your soul's cry

Together soul power can be more than an ethnic slogan

It can be a transformative place of residence where all creation that yearns

to be placed can have a home

I want to ground the hate of this world into the ignorance abyss it belongs

in

I want to provide an attraction that the beauty of my Divine's creation

cannot resist

I want to be the Gravity that my lost heart once only had hoped for

But can now clearly see

The Power to pull my fellow human into a place of their own destiny's

making

I want that power, I need that power, I will submit to that power

I want to be Gravity

Anthony Brown-2015

CHAPTER 4

PURPOSE

The Joy of Knowing the Why!

Purpose is more concerned with the **"What"** and **"How"** than the **"Why"**. The thing is people are always more happy to know the latter than receive and submit to the former. It is mankind's addiction. We're not addicted to receiving Sam's Love. We, as humans, aren't naturally drawn to the power that resonates from it or inherently open to its direction. The power that comes from having a conscious choice in life confuses purpose when, in actuality, choice was created to amplify love through affirmation and directivity. Sam loves us. Choice was given to us for one reason...for us to choose to love him back. That's it.

The reason we inhabit space in this body we call the universe is to love. Love is the current that moves all things in the universe through their natural cycle of transformation and gives them meaning and intent. Sam's intent is to Love, His power emanates from Love, and purpose is the clothing Love wears, not an individualistic ideal to aspire to for personal gain or affirmation. Purpose is God loving us and us loving Him…that's it. Love encompasses the nature, character and action of God because Love is God. We are made up of it. We are a physical manifestation of the nuance of the Love of God, like everything else in creation. How I look, what I wear, what I do, my direction in life and the decisions I make all are expressions of Love's nuance shining through my being. I have purpose. I know the **"Why"** in that purpose. It is to love Sam. If everyone and everything is a part of Sam than my purpose is to love everyone and everything. If Sam's love is like a current of electricity, let's say the universe's current of transformative power, than my purpose is to keep that current flowing in its prescribed direction. If Sam's love is to manifest in the form of a statement through the lens of who I am, I have to be grounded first. Then I have to provide focus so Sam can channel His Love through the lens of my love, amplifying that statement's power through my expression. Once it is amplified through the love that is me its purpose is defined through me, because I become the clothing for that loves expression. I define its purpose. Now when people see me they see the purpose of that love. Not just another wandering soul with no connectivity, who isn't sure what his or her purpose is. Then I speak the statement given. Maybe it's "Good Morning". Maybe it's "Everything in your life is going to get better". Maybe it's "Get off your ass and make something out of your fucked up existence". The words don't mean anything without the power of Love behind them. Words are just vehicles for power. If they are empty, no matter what their form is, no effectivity will be generated by them. Our purpose as human's is to love Sam by being amplifiers of His Love and Grace on this earth and universally. Grace is an understanding, not a force. The understanding that we are all one. If a man murders your son his action ripples through all eternity. It hurts everyone because everyone manifested from the same source, we are all one organism. In this he didn't just falter, but the whole entire organism suffered a loss of purpose. Your son isn't gone because no one has the power to destroy love, but actions can change its form and expression. Your son is gone in his present physical expression but he lives on in a different form, sometimes in a different dimension of time and space. Even scientist believe that energy is never destroyed, that it just changes forms. Even Christian's believe that a soul is never lost but goes on to rest and manifest in a different realm after leaving this one. The concept of punishment in reality, spirituality, or any other form is based in the assumption that something or someone is eternally lost and the catalyst or responsible person for that loss deserves an accountable reckoning for that. The truth is we don't have that much power. Creation is cyclical, which is to say it cycles from one form of manifestation to another. All loss is temporary. All forms of remorse as a result of that loss are based in emotion and sentiment. This definitely serves a healing purpose but is by nature and design temporary. Anyone who harbors emotional pain, distress, fear, or resentment past its appointed time is doing so by choice.

Our purpose is to love one another in our own unique way as expressed through who we are. Christ said that our purpose is to love one another as He loved us. Could it really be that simple? Yes it can. The message of His sacrifice is to teach us that after taking on all the sin of the entire world we are still to love in return because that is who we are. We carry the manifest presence of God's love on the Earth. The choice to love is the choice to amplify the truth of Sam's presence in your life and everyone else's. The joy of knowing the "Why" in your life is the joy of knowing

Him. Knowing Him is knowing your purpose. All creation knows this truth because it is made up of it.

The **"What"** is the raw purpose you receive from Sam. The **"How"** are the necessary steps in that purpose needed to see it succeed. The power that comes from your focus drives your soul's imperative. This translates into the passion your mind needs to act on the steps prescribed to carry out your purpose's requirement. This brings a result or manifest destiny. In this book, I don't want to express a radical new way of thinking. I don't want to reinvent the wheel or start a new movement. I simply want to connect people to the understanding that living is an organic and wonderful experience, not a laborious one. Studying the simple doesn't lead to freedom of living. Society's constant search for reality in the complex doesn't result in contentment, just greater questions and in some cases more confusion. How we relate to and deal with each other as humans and creation in general is my concern because we all share a planet that needs our balance and attention, not our strife and division. If we all knew our purpose, focused more on submitting to its vision, and walked out the necessary steps to its manifestation, more could

be revealed to us a lot quicker.

Drunk in love

Man, I can't think

This can't be it because I can't think

I just told the dude on my right I love him

For no fuckin reason at all!

I kissed the woman on my left, said I couldn't help it

She slapped me, felt so good

I then apologized to her husband, I didn't know people!

He laughed and I bought him a beer

Well, he threatened to kicked my ass first, then I bought him a beer

Then he laughed and we talked for an hour

I'm Black, he's Latino…we hate each other right?

We don't though…I knocked on the bathroom shit-stall because I heard

the splash

"You ok bro?"

He's like "I love your disrespectful ass man, I'm good"

I saw my wife, she was way pissed…said that's it

I said let's have a drink first then I'll sign the papers bitch

Man I was out of line

But after the Chardonnay she say's

I introduced you to the elixir of the God's and you shit on me Tony

I'm like, you know I love you baby, I'm just an asshole sometimes

She kissed my undeserving ass and told me to come home soon

I drink another shot, the world looks better

The lady I kissed thanks me for checking on her husband, says that she

hasn't been able to get such a rise out of him in years

Then tells me he just fucked her in the bathroom he puked in

I'm like not on top of the same stall right?

We both laughed our ass off

Now I see 2 kids in the bar

They can't be more than 8 to 12 years old

These boys say to me…"look at this monkey in this bar, acting like a

fuckin fool"

I laughed my ass off

The language, the hate…the discontent

I started makin monkey sounds and scared these little idiots out of the bar

Too young to be in a bar anyway

Dad walks in and makes them apologize, the kids are crying

Because he beat their ass probably

I'm like dude why did you do that, they're just being stupid like I was at

their age

I'm just glad they're safe

We are all from one tribe bro, the human tribe

The boys start crying more, they say that some crazy dude snatched them

up while their dad was using the bathroom at Target and took them to this

bar

He was crazy, telling them he would kill them if they spoke out

Then he saw me and asked them what they saw when they looked at me

They said a black man

He said "No kids that's a fuckin monkey and if you don't call him that

Imma kill you both!"

Pops is like I've been looking for my boy's for the last 45 minutes

I begged God to help me find them

Some people saw me praying then ran to me and told me that they had

seen two boys that seemed to be in distress

Told me they came in here with some dude that looked off

When you made those monkey sounds it spooked the guy and he ran out

the bar

My kids heard me calling for them from outside and ran out to meet me

You saved my kids life bro, I love you bro

He bought my drunk ass another beer

One Love

Anthony Brown-2015

CHAPTER 5

ACT

Acting on Love's Imperative

Like a tree reaches up for the sunlight with each branch and down with its roots for every drop of water, absorbing every mineral to nourish its strength. Our actions are like branches reaching out in time and space to grasp a hold of destiny's end, its result.

I take my actions serious. They are the mental and physical manifestation of my love's inspiration in this realm and dimension. If I give a woman flowers to impress, when those flowers die the impression fades. They are a wonderful gesture but they resonate at a low level of endurance. If I hear a woman tell me about the kitchen sink, how every time she runs the s faucet it shakes and spews brown water and I don't respond I just missed an opportunity. To act on her heart's imperative would have been to fix it. Her action was to share something with me that was embarrassing and distressing to her. My action was to fix that faucet so every time she turns on the water its clarity and peaceful flow reminds her that I am useful, I am handy. My goal is to provide clarity and peace to whatever I touch. Men, whether you get it or not, a woman will reward you if you fix the sink. Flowers only guarantee a smile and a pleasant comment. A man whose action can meet and satisfy the heart of a woman's need will get every ounce of nectar sucked out of his personal faucet. Now that I have the men's, as well as the women's attention, let's go deeper.

The action is your conscious mental and physical demonstration of your mind's passionate command. Every purpose has steps that are to be acted on. The key is to act in the timeframe that the step's instruction commands. Acting is about timing.

In a play you have a role. You are the killer in a play about that killer's life and experiences in murder. You have to come out and stab a women in act two right after she says "Kenneth I love you". You decide you're going to spice things up and go your own way. You're still going to act in the way instructed, but you feel it would be more dynamic to do it in an earlier scene when the woman says, "I'm afraid for my life and I don't want to get you killed Kenneth!". You make your move and damn you feel good. The issue is that the murder is supposed to happen while the woman is writing a letter to Kenneth. She professes her love while she's writing. She's thinking out loud so the audience can participate. You move into strike when Kenneth is actually physically present with her. Now he sees you coming and instead of saying "I can protect you Amy" he says, "What the fuck bro!" Now the audience starts to laugh because this scene is supposed to take place during the eighteenth century in England! You ruined the whole play. *When* you act is paramount.

You grounded yourself, focused, and received the amplified power from Sam, which articulated your purpose. You have drive to feed your soul's imperative. It translated into passion to fuel your mind's determination. Now all that was left to do was act on your mind's clear commands from its defined purpose. This is where so many of us miss the mark. The steps in our actions have an optimal time for execution. When we miss our appointed time our purpose's end result is sabotaged. Prepare for the job interview, dress to impress, freshen the breath, but if you're late you're not going to be received or heard. That's on us, no one to blame but the man or woman in the mirror.

There are many dimensions of results. In my introduction I gave the ice cream example. I focused on the ice cream. What if it wasn't about ice cream, what if it was about meeting my next client at that location of 7-Eleven? What if it was about me saving a child from choking on a rubbery 7-Eleven hot dog? What if I was a single woman, who always was unlucky in love, and Jay Z's tour manager decided to stop in and buy a slushy? What if he stopped in when I was supposed to be there? I'm at my normal location, pissed because the store manager defrosted the freezer an hour ago and all the ice cream got ruined. He got busy with customers and hasn't even updated the prices for the ice cream yet, which happens to be on sale. If you think my example is about you getting Jay Z's autograph you'd be wrong.

It's about the fact that I went to High School with Darryl. I dated him for a year and a half and was in love with the dude. Our paths took us in different directions in life but I loved this man and he loved me too. Jay Z had a concert in Long Beach, and afterwards, had his way with a groupie. She lives in San Pedro. So he had his tour manager, Darryl, drop her off and he got thirsty so now he's at 7-Eleven. I'm supposed to be there but I know what's best for me. I finally come to my senses and go there but by the time I arrive, the Maybach's leaving the parking lot. I say, "Damn that's a nice car" because at this time in my life I've turned to more shallow pursuits as true love keeps alluding me. My man was in that car and I didn't even know it! Timing is everything people. Act when you're told to act.

I shouldn't have to become a fine-ass sista for you to get the point. I shouldn't keep blaming society for my troubles and failures. I don't believe life has to be as hard as we make it. Victim mentality streams out of the consciousness of a man that doesn't know how to seize opportunity with action when it presents itself. What confuses us is that everything we act on brings a result but it's not a pure, powerful or transformational result when we miss our timing. The result that your destiny craves is predicated upon you following the steps your purpose requires purely, without resistance, and in its appointed window of time. I have told my clients, on many occasions, that an action I prescribed for them to face a challenge was no longer valid because they didn't act when they were supposed to. I tell them they missed their window of opportunity for the best result. I then have to come up with a whole different set of intuitive instruction to guide them to their desired end. Usually it takes longer. Then they get upset because memory is short when it comes to personal resistance. They don't remember that it took longer because they resisted plan A. They are stuck on how long it took for plan B to work. I have to laugh inside.

I'm a plan **<u>A</u>** kind of guy. We should adopt the first answer that comes from our spiritual intuition and instinct as it carries the most power. This fuels our soul's drive with the power needed to fuel our mind's passion which in turn results in determination. Now we clearly follow the steps of our answer's assigned purpose and submit to the appropriate time window for its directed action. This **"<u>Action</u>"** in its purity, resonant with amplified power, sufficient drive, and clarified passion…leads to our desired result. In short, follow plan **<u>A</u>!**

I'm diving in

I'm breathing heavy

I'm feeling the sweat roll down the side of my cheek

I see what I want

Know what I need

Then I stop

Because the emotion is too deep

The wall of patience I think, too steep

She's never gonna cum

She's so stuck in her mind, her passions on the run

Then

I caught her in a kiss

It extends to a thigh grip

Now every aspiration of her misty breath, I won't miss

I hear it…feel it…sense it

My awareness, the bulb is finally lit

I touch, no not yet

Stroke, almost

Just keep kissing her

Don't move until her body tells you too

Now

Taste like you're at your favorite winery

Taste, savor, taste, savor

Follow that pattern

Now there's a slight shake…

It's being subdued, my tongue is numb

Stop

Look at her…then

It's time to get really hungry

Eat…it's time to eat

An earthquake just took you to the one place where it can't destroy

To the heavenly realm of a woman's passionate mind

As it speaks her whole body follows the pattern of its musical artistry

You just sang a song…she just sang back

Anthony Brown-2015

CHAPTER 6

RESULTS

Manifest Destiny

The result. Why a chapter on what seems to be a self-explanatory concept? Because how we handle the manifestation of following Sam's vision for us defines our character. How we handle success opens up a clear pathway for more of the same. This chapter is about humility and thanksgiving. Smelling the roses isn't a part of The Destiny Cycle. Humbling yourself as you see lives change around you is, especially if that life is your own. Self-awareness is key for manifesting your destiny. Self-awareness comes from understanding that we all our one, articulated in a unique spirit, manifested from Love. Selfishness is necessary because in order to follow our path we need to make sure our mind's passion is fed by the proper spiritual nutrients from our soul's drive. Our body needs the proper physical sustainment in the form of the earth's bounty of water, fruits, vegetables, grains and protein. Being self-serving however, sabotages our purposed outcome because it is focused on personal gain instead of giving.

The result is how you share your gift with the world and its response to it. When I coach the result is what gives me the most joy. Seeing a client's life change for the better. Feeling their energy shift into a more self-supportive resonance. The results tell me that the work I'm doing has validity and manifests whatever intent its purpose dictated. Without a result that reflects my client's vision and aspiration, there is no efficacy to my work.

I give dating advice to my male clients. Their favorite sentiment to express when I tell them what to do for success is, "You're bullshitting right?" My advice is almost always counterintuitive to how they were brought up and what they were taught was appropriate for masculine behavior and communication with women. What keeps them coming back to me are the results. My results are the reason I am still relevant in this work, even though most haven't heard of me up until now. My clients know that when I tell them what to do and they follow my instructions exactly, the results they want manifest.

The point is not the success. The success is part of a cycle of manifestation that repeats itself over and over again. You shouldn't live in any one part of the Destiny Cycle for too long because then it becomes a place of rest and hiding. Some people get stuck in the results phase. "Look what I did" should not be every other statement that comes out of your mouth. At the same time don't be too busy acting on instructions to savor the journey or so immersed in the wonder of your purpose that you render yourself inefficient. The results represent your manifest destiny, your ability and capacity to follow through on Love's inspiration and the result of its action revealed. People should look at your result and say, "Wow…what am I called to do in this life?"

I'm empty. The Destiny Cycle has been laid out in clarity and I have peace of mind about it. I understand some may say, "How do I really tune into this? It's so foreign to me." I have felt a special connection to Sam since I was a child. I have had the gift of spiritual insight for as long as I can remember. I process what I hear like breathing and instinctively act on its prerogative and protocol, at least it feels that way. Of course I make mistakes, miss the mark often, and get lost from time to time. Even though I have a gift there's also a development aspect to it, a practice that can be duplicated. Following one's spiritual instinct and intuition are an imperative for a directed life, not a fantasy or wishful notion.

I'm going to address this in the last chapter because I want everyone who reads this book to feel that the principles are accessible and easily duplicated. Success comes from the practice of acting on the inspired vision of your soul's passionate imperative. For the conscious mind to receive the soul's inspired spiritual vision purely, the gateway of your spiritual instinct and intuition have to be open and clear of obstruction.

Spotlight on me

So many beautiful new things in this life

Spotlight on you

Thank you for making me believe in hope again

Spotlight on them

Their music made me want to live again

Spotlight on God

He changed my way of thinking

I used to…abolish that thought

I want to…taking it out of my mind's power

I need to…not really

I have to…

Love unconditionally

Feed generously

Take everything

Give everything

Feel everything

Live everyday

Steal back all my time lost

Receive my Divine's loving treasure

By diving into His castle's throne room

I want him to change me, instruct me, and release me

My existence is the result of His time and attention filtered through my

soul's imperative

Reflecting His divine love's ability to transform my life into its beautiful

end result

Anthony Brown-2015

CHAPTER 7

SPIRITUAL INSTINCT AND INTUITION

See it coming from a Mile Away

When you enter into a relationship with your whole heart whether it be a business relationship, contract relationship, or intimate one your heart represents your vulnerability, your unguarded true self. To live in the Destiny Cycle requires you to keep your heart open and receptive to the Love of Sam and your mind resilient against the criticism of others.

The power of your own personal vision and focus can't be underestimated. You are your own deliverance, you are your own guide, the church of Jesus Christ lives inside of you, and the power to transform your life is within you. The angst you feel, it's not from this world, or from outside pressure or influence. Your spirit wants to live. It wants to give back to universe that spawned its existence. It wants to love or should I say it wants to relate because it is love. Spiritual intuition and instinct comes from the heart of who you are. A spiritual being living in a body of stone, flesh and sexual identity. The stone represents this society's construct: the Matrix of belief systems, ideals, idioms, and programing that have been constructed to keep us down. As in looking down, reaching down, pulling down and putting down. Down has a universal representation of oppressive force. Gravity holds us in place, but a suffocating ideology pulls are spirit down from flight. Flight is a universal symbol of freedom. When we see birds fly we feel free, the action gives us hope that even in this world of oppressive concepts and religious bigotry we can still fly. We try to duplicate the act through technology instead of getting the real message. Our spirit wants to fly, to express its true reason for being. The reason is to love, because we all are made up of love. We are love manifested in cells of blood, bone, cartilage, traveling through water. Water is our physical life's medium. It is representative of the essence that directs our flow in life. Water flows, transforms, and makes paths for our spirit to travel through. The waters of the spirit of who we are. Spiritual intuition is the way we let Sam's water wash over and cleanse our minds illusion and erosion with universal truth.

You get an idea, a great one. You're going to go into the oil business by fracking the earth of this precious resource. You develop the patents for the technology needed, project the astronomical profits, and plan to act on your technologies merit. As the waters wash over your brilliant mind you see a vision. You see the earth cracking, the animals in it dying, and people's lives being transformed for the worse. You see the pain, the suffering, the price humanity will pay for this idea. On the other side is money... The life that money affords. You're not poor but you certainly aren't rich. The temptation is so great. The technology so practical for harvesting a resource that is beyond accepted. But the spirit of the earth cries out to your own spirit and says "Don't do this." That's your Spiritual intuition talking. You don't listen because the voice of money is louder.

I'm looking at a documentary about fracking and I see scenes that horrify me. People are running their sinks and setting the same sink water on fire because it's so polluted as a result of this practice. The water of spiritual intuition that runs over your mind's greed is being set afire because of your decision. It still flows but no one should drink it now. Because it's polluted with this world's greed instead of resonating with the life force that comes from God himself.

It's time to listen to the real you. But how is that done? By following what you know and being who you are. Sam's love brings life, not destruction. Knowing comes from life experience and demonstrating wisdom and clarity in your decisions. If you grow a plant with water and sunlight then it stands to reason that if you take both elements away it will wither and die. The simple shouldn't be complicated. If you understand that you are a walking manifestation of God's love then loving action should be an instinctual prerogative, not an unimaginable goal. Here is where religious and scientific doctrine comes in and define our expression for us. Religion says that we have to accept a man or woman's person based on belief, not natural prerogative. Every natural prerogative we have today is filtered through society's religious and scientific sensibility. Science deals with natural law, but is very limited in its scope and dimension because it relies on perceptions that are predicated and defined by human potential. The assumption is that we are the smartest, most evolved creatures in the universe and have the best understanding of how that universe functions and exists. This neither represents, defines nor amplifies our natural inclination. Assuming I am an evil, judgmental, destructive force of nature that needs subduing doesn't lend itself to freedom of expression. It is only slavery to a construct designed to restrain us from a pre-determined destructive end. Thinking my mind's eye is more evolved than any other aware form of intelligence is absurd. Scientists don't even believe that spiritual intuition and instinct exist.

I know things, I don't know why I know them. I hear things…the things I hear manifest into reality and seldom are connected to my reach or influence.

I was holding my cell phone and texting. I was texting a dear friend and I saw a picture pop up on my screen in the text stream. It was a picture I had taken years back from a professional photographer. My first sense was that my friend had texted the picture to me. I saw the pic for about three to five seconds and then it disappeared. I asked my friend if she had texted me this picture. She said she hadn't. I described the picture, what I was wearing and the context for it. I had sent it to her years back and was curious as to why she had texted it to me. I thought this up until it disappeared before my eyes. She seemed stunned. She told me that she was thinking of me and had been looking at that very picture about 10 minutes prior to my text regarding it. It was one of her favorite

pictures of me. I saw a picture appear and then disappear in the text

stream of my cell phone, one of me that I had taken years prior, that my

friend had been gazing at 10 minutes before I inquired about it. I saw into

a different dimension of time and space and my friend verified it. I have

many examples of this sort of thing in my life. Your belief or disbelief

doesn't in anyway make it more or less real for me. It simply is. Spiritual

intuition comes out of that place. It can't be explained in natural or

scientific terms. It is the fleeting thought a new mother has to check on

her baby and when she does she sees her son or daughter is choking and

needs help. Why did she think to check then? It's the urging that

instinctually moves you to another seat on the bus and when the accident

comes, the place you would have been sitting gets smashed in and you

realize you would have died if you stayed there. It's the way a woman

knows when a man is lying when he's actually telling the truth in context,

but is living a deeper lie in his overall life. And when a woman is lying to

you about her whereabouts because she's planning a surprise birthday

party but in actuality is living in a deeper truth, which is that she loves you

and is willing to do anything to set you apart and show you that love…even with her deceptive act. You can be right but wrong, wrong

but just, and happy in pain. It's about where your soul is resonating in any

action. The action itself doesn't define your character as much as where

you are in the universe during that action's demonstration. You're

spiritual intuition tells you where to stand and how to act in a given

situation. Your spiritual instinct is how your mind and intellect respond

naturally to your spiritual intuition's request.

A child is playing in the bathroom of a crowded restaurant and

someone comes in and pulls out a gun and says he's looking for his ex-

wife Susan. He says that he's going to kill her and his daughter and that

he's going to kill one person every five minutes until his wife shows

herself. Before anyone can lie and say she's not in the restaurant Susan

appears from underneath a table. She doesn't want to see anyone else be

killed on her account. Then he asks where their daughter Terry is. Terry's

in the bathroom, she's only 8. John was having his afternoon coffee after

a long hard day on the docks that started at 5:30 AM. He sees this

scenario unfolding in his favorite diner and is horrified. John has 5 kids,

one of which is his youngest daughter. She's 8 years old. He saw Terry run into the bathroom to use it with her favorite doll in hand. She took her

doll Maggie everywhere with her to ease her nerves and make her feel

safe. It is clear to John that the man holding up the diner is mentally

unstable and unpredictable. Terry starts making playful noises from the

bathroom and her crazed father hears it. He say's "Come out..." Just

then, John says, "Sir, Sir please don't call my daughter out of the

bathroom, please don't hurt my daughter". John starts screaming over and

over again for the man not to hurt his daughter. The crazed man looks at

John and tells him to shut the fuck up. He runs out the diner with his ex-

wife. John runs into the women's bathroom and startles Terry. He calms

her down and asks if she has a cell phone. He explains calmly that her

mommy and daddy went away to talk for a while and left him to take care

of her. He calls 911 and gets the police on the line. He explains the

situation and says that Terry's mother's contact info was in her phone.

The police use the <u>Find my I-phone</u> app that Susan has downloaded on her

phone and they track her. They are later able to talk down Susan's crazy

ex and take him into custody. The news later interviews John and asks

him how he came up with the idea to distract the man by saying Susan's daughter was his. John simply said, "She is my daughter, and I didn't want to see her or her mother die".

John was Susan's second husband. It didn't work out between them but John never let that little girl's love leave his heart. His ex-step daughter wasn't that at all, she was his heart.

When we realize that titles are just that, only identifiers. The essence of our connection with others is love and compassion. Spiritual intuition and instinct has only one imperative in the human soul, to connect the love of one with the love of another. When we act in this love we live above ourselves as mere citizens and transcend to become guardians of Love's imperative. We promote life and not death in all our actions. Death is inevitable, but the premature death of Love's manifestation can't be tolerated by loving human beings.

If you're honest with yourself then you'll acknowledge that spiritual intuition and instinct are a more natural state to be in than society's bird cage of repression and slavery. A "successful" society works when the rules are followed and everyone stays within their prescribed place of residence and assigned habit. I like the word community better. I know it's just a word but it resonates because a community at its best is a group of loving members moving in harmony toward a goal of one-ness and progress. I don't want society's vision of "utopia." I want to live in a community that reflects and radiates the love of the Divine, and the love of one soul to another.

I hear you

I feel you

I'm surrounded by you

But the pigs keep oinking

The cats keep hissing

My wife keeps dissing

And my children keep missing…

The Point

I need a sale

A discount on life's commitment

With a sip of Apple Ale

The GPS has a glitch

I know the way

But still want to fix this bitch

Remember when we knew phone numbers by heart

And names weren't an exclusion of our brains capacity?

And cell phones weren't smart

I just had a feeling about things

No need to use lube to jimmy myself into the wrong space

Adaptable to change, enjoying everything life brings

Now I see the glass half empty, and it costs too much to fill it back up

My cynical steps taking me ever closer to the end

Of an undirected life

That society has rewarded me for… so much

I feel empty inside

I want to know in my gut…this is where I should walk

I want my heart to feel good after I talk

I want to look at my son with pride

Maybe I reach out one last time

To my past's wonder

And catch back up to my joy's stride

I used to see things coming

Let me let the evening news die

And embrace the hope of a new day in my life

Once again

Anthony Brown-2015

SUMMATION

I realize that these concepts have fuller application. I have been teaching, living and breathing them for a while now and can actually sum them up in about 5 minutes verbally. I know they work, but how that manifests for each individual will be unique and different. I'm going to summarize them now so that the reader can apply them practically, not just in a literary sense. As these principles are lived in day to day life they will demonstrate their worth in more ways than a book, workshop or even one-on-one coaching can encapsulate. I give all these options as vehicles for concept absorption. The ultimate demonstration of validity for this system is daily use in an open and imaginative way. I look forward to great testimonies of victories achieved and deliverances experienced.

The principles of the Destiny Cycle were not created by me. I believe they are as organic as life itself. I released them in a way that my spirit's inspiration dictated. This is to say I wrote The Destiny Cycle as a result of operating in the principles of the Destiny Cycle. I walked this out myself as I was writing this book which is kind of amazing to me and my clients are experiencing great success in their lives from doing the same.

This is a workbook and the principles laid out are to be acted upon. I suggest anyone reading this book walk out the steps in the cycle for any goal or affirmation they choose to apply it to and gauge their own results honestly and without jadedness. If so done, the end product, I believe, will be amazing.

The Destiny Cycle…

Grounded - Understand that God and your uniquely assigned spirit love you. You are to give love, receive love, and be love. Plant your feet on the ground and feel your body root itself like a tree. Take two or three deep breaths. Feel yourself at peace…you'll recognize this feeling as your mind will clear and you'll be ready to focus on whatever aspiration or goal you have.

Focus - Visualize the sun as your source. See yourself as a lens, absorb the sun's essence through you and channel that powerful beam to land on the purpose of your affirmation or goal.

Power- The power that is created from your spirit's translation and reception of Sam's Love and power through the lens of who you are. This power is specifically designed to feed your soul's imperative and becomes the drive necessary to feed your conscious mind's passion.

Purpose- The clear vision that your conscious mind sees from your soul's imperative. It became directed power from your focus, and now is translated into sufficient drive, fueling your mind's passion. Within this vision are the steps that are necessary to walk out your affirmation or goal's original inspiration with purity.

Act- Taking appropriate action at the appointed time, on your mind's vision. The body follows the mind with a pure purpose from clear commands that are driven by passion.

Results - You will manifest the destiny of whatever your affirmation or original goal's intent was.

www.ingramcontent.com/pod-product-compliance
Lightning Source LLC
Chambersburg PA
CBHW051737040426
42447CB00008B/1178